THINK³ᴰ
PERSONAL   PROFESSIONAL   POTENTIAL

TAMIEN DYSART and VANEY HARIRI

Copyright © 2016 by Tamien Dysart and Vaney Hariri

ISBN: 978-1-945255-03-8

All rights reserved. No part of this book may be reproduced or transmitted in any form or by any means, electronic or mechanical, including photocopying, recording or by any information storage and retrieval system, without permission in writing from the copyright owner. For information on distribution rights, royalties, derivative works or licensing opportunities on behalf of this content or work, please contact the publisher at the address below.

Printed in the United States of America.

Although the author and publisher have made every effort to ensure that the information and advice in this book was correct and accurate at press time, the author and publisher do not assume and hereby disclaim any liability to any party for any loss, damage, or disruption caused from acting upon the information in this book or by errors or omissions, whether such errors or omissions result from negligence, accident, or any other cause.

Throne Publishing Group
2329 N Career Ave #215
Sioux Falls, SD 57107
ThronePG.com

THINK³ᴰ
PERSONAL   PROFESSIONAL   POTENTIAL

A Radically New Approach
To Maximizing the Potential of Your Team

THRONE
PUBLISHING GROUP

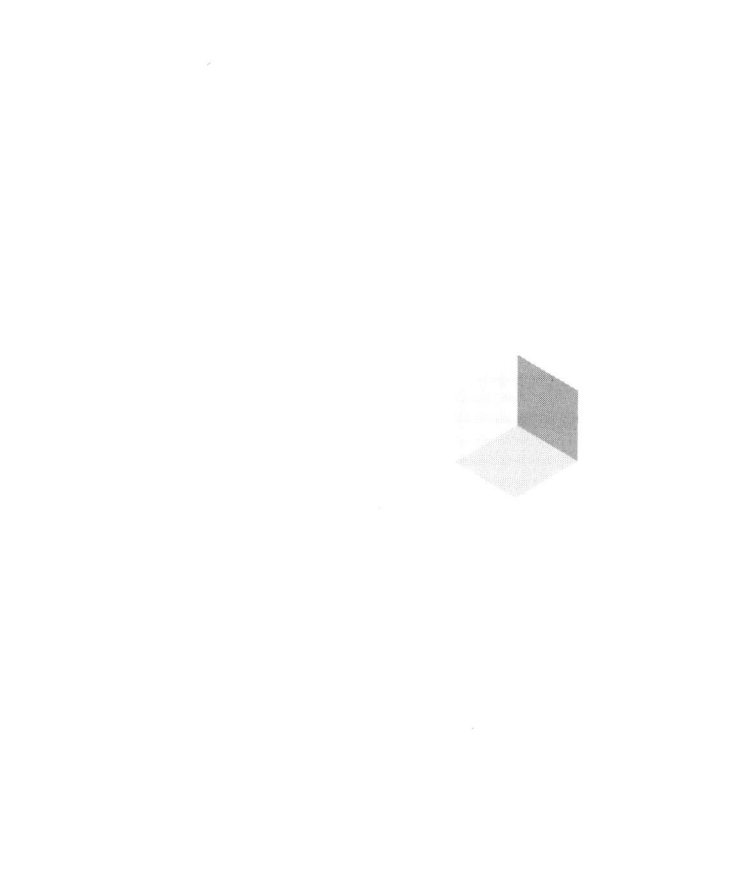

Table of Contents

Introduction		6
CHAPTER 1	Think 3D	14
CHAPTER 2	Something to Believe In	28
CHAPTER 3	Attitude = Altitude	38
CHAPTER 4	The Eco-System	54
CHAPTER 5	After You!	68
CHAPTER 6	Do You See What I See?	86
CHAPTER 7	...But Can You Do It Again?	96
Conclusion	Why Not?	110

INTRODUCTION

There is a reason you picked up this book.

When you pause and reflect on the current state of your work environment, would you automatically rate your job satisfaction at a ten? Something inside you says there is more to be had than the current day-to-day repetition you call your work life, but you are unsure about what it is. Or maybe you've even gone as far as settling, thinking this is just the way it is because you aren't sure what, if anything, can be done about it.

Or maybe your current realization of your situation is already blatant to you. You have recognized the need for change in your workplace. Employees around you seem to be going through the motions every day. Engagement has taken a noticeable dive. There's a stagnant feel to how people interact with each other.

People feel distracted all week, holding out for Friday. Then they waste half their weekends worrying about Monday. Employees go home exhausted and wake up each morning with a feeling of dread.

Whether or not it is admitted, it's clear retention is down and hiring budgets are up. The dreams of "doing what you love" and "company loyalty" seem like outdated fantasies of older generations.

But what needs to change? What *can* be changed? Are we to really just accept that riding the Ferris wheel of our working lives is something to settle for, and we should simply take it on the chin and not disrupt the flow as it's been sold to us?

This book is not a wake-up call. Whether you're a leader in your workplace or an employee chances are you already see the need for something new, if you do a true, deep-dive evaluation of your workplace. But rethinking job satisfaction isn't like studying a quarterly report. The topic of job satisfaction and its impact within a business isn't a new field of study. But what we're talking about goes deeper than the surface, two-way relationship between job satisfaction and productivity. This is new territory. Before a business can move forward, it needs to step back and find its current location.

If success is a map, then consider this book the "you are here" marker.

Business is complicated. Like any large airport or mall, there are a multitude of places to go. It's easy to get lost in your attempt to get to your destination. There's nothing wrong with checking the map now and then. But before you can move forward, it helps to know where you are first.

Every workday is filled with decisions that determine where a company is headed. No two businesses are the same and none of them have quite the same challenges or goals. But one thing every company deals with is change.

One of the biggest changes to modern business in recent years has been its workforce. They've been called Millennials, Generations Y and Z, and Centennials. Traditional employers may see these characteristics and assume this age group is selfish, spoiled, or lazy.

This demonstrates a fundamental lack of understanding many employers have for current job hunters. Every generation holds fast to its own values and beliefs.

After all, every successful company that has survived several years or decades of business has done so by adapting to the changing environment. Yet the idea that employees should adapt to evolving business environments without expecting their working conditions to change as well is absurd.

These capable and talented people want something different than what companies gave their parents. Understanding what motivates employees and harnessing it is the difference between stagnation and real success.

Whether or not businesses want to face the facts or not, the facts still remain. Studies[1] have shown that the percentage of employees worldwide that are either unengaged or actively unengaged in their day-to-day jobs ranges from 70% or higher. What is the true cost of this to a business?

Now, common sense would ask the question, with statistics like these having been available for quite some time, why are more businesses not creating strategies to bridge this gap?

This isn't to say that many companies aren't aware of the issue or that they haven't tried to address this growing epidemic. The reality of doing business adds layers of complexity, meaning there isn't a simple solution. With any company there are always shifting priorities demanding immediate attention, which often leaves very

---

[1] Adkins, Amy. "Majority of U.S. Employees Not Engaged Despite Gains in 2014." Gallup.com. Gallup, 28 Jan. 2015. Web. 03 May 2016.

Crabtree, Steve. "Worldwide, 13% of Employees Are Engaged at Work." Gallup.com. Gallup, 8 Oct. 2013. Web. 03 May 2016.

See Modern Survey: http://www.modernsurvey.com/fall2014

little time to effectively drive engagement and build a sustainable, dynamic culture. It is an impossibility to successfully chart any course of direction without first finding your "you are here" marker on the map.

So how long do you go on ignoring the tumor? We get regular checkups to ensure we're positioning ourselves to stay healthy in the years ahead. We have our vehicles routinely checked to keep them maintained and running at their optimal level. We even do scheduled financial reviews of our business to keep everything in order, to prevent surprises, and to look for opportunities to maximize our profits. So why not with culture?

So let's talk about how you can get the most out of Think 3D.

> "A culture will emerge whether intended or not, but if it's not one you invest in, it will certainly be one that you pay for."

There are countless business models out there that will tell you how to be successful. If you're like us, you know success is more than just a paycheck and a 3% annual raise. Things need to change around the office. But the reality is that permanent change takes regular maintenance. It takes checkups and reviews. It takes intent.

Think broadly for a moment over your life to date. Have you ever accomplished anything of significance without the power of absolute intention behind you? It doesn't matter if the goal is dieting and exercise, going after a promotion, or starting a business, it takes real intention to propel you toward the goal you're after.

True intention to change, however, cannot occur if we don't believe there is a problem. This is the danger for the majority, and consequently, the result is mediocrity. Many people start out motivated and will sell you on their intention, but the subsequent action fades once the reality of overcoming the obstacles sets in.

People attend conferences all of the time and are motivated in the moment, but then find themselves the same person a week later. Businesses invest in speakers or retreats to help spark their employees' performance, but without a strategy of sustaining it over time, reverting back to the familiar is the end result.

The reality is that all diets work, but not if *you* don't. Every piece of exercise equipment works, but if *you* don't put forth the consistent effort to maximize its potential results over a sustained period of time, you'll never reap the benefits

What is your intent? The knowledge you gain here will be useless unless your intention is to use it. To cultivate success in yourself, you need to do something different. To improve your workplace culture, you need to find or locate your coworkers' "you are here" markers.

As you read each chapter, picture what that change will look like. Create a game plan to make Thinking 3D a reality in your workplace. And along the way, ask yourself three questions:

1. **What do you have to gain?**

2. **What do you have to lose?**

3. and most importantly:
Why not?

CHAPTER 1

THINK 3D

You know a successful business when you see it. And yet, business success is such a vague term to define. When we try to measure a company's performance, we usually look for signs such as brand recognition, product and service reviews, and sales and stock market value.

After all, the strength of a company's finances and business savvy define its success, right? Or is there more to the story here?

When most people start job hunting, they aren't looking for a successful employer so much as a *good* one. Their criteria are substantially different. Job hunters look at salary, benefits, work environment, and employee satisfaction. This means that the way employers measure themselves is different than how new—or even prospective—employees see them.

THE FALLACY OF PAY[2]

Why did they leave? According to a Gallup study, at least 75% of the reasons for voluntary turnover can be influenced by managers. They leave because they are not happy, but don't take a new job unless they find the money. Most exit surveys fail to capture the true reason someone left. People don't quit jobs, they quit the environment; they quit the *people*. The people that create the culture. Rather than focusing on why they left, the better question to ask is this: What drove them to even look?

---

[2] Sorenson, Susan. "How Employee Engagement Drives Growth." Gallup.com. Gallup, 20 June 2013. Web. 03 May 2016.

To be a business that's genuinely considered both *successful* and *attractive* to employees, there are two dimensions of growth within your workforce you must focus on, the professional and the potential dimensions, or what we call the two-dimensional business model.

A company's professional dimension involves its day-to-day operations. This includes skill training, facilities and equipment, communication resources, and anything else that allows employees to perform their jobs effectively.

The potential dimension focuses less on a company's daily functions and more on its employees' career paths. A stable business knows how to invest in its workforce by introducing programs that help to mentor and develop leaders within their ranks. Simply put, the professional and potential dimensions of any good company equip its employees with the tools and advancement needed for both to succeed.

This is nothing new to most business owners, and the two-dimensional model looks relatively fool-proof on paper. After all, this business model is widely accepted by some of the largest and most successful companies on the planet. And yet, statistics show that around 70% or more of employees worldwide report a lack of active engagement and satisfaction at their jobs.

So what's missing from this equation? If a company invests in coaching and promoting its workforce, shouldn't their employees be more fulfilled?

What many employers overlook is the need to inspire their workforce.

Imagine the difference between an employee who simply does their job and someone who comes to work each day with a genuine desire to excel at what they do. Not only does the latter add more value to the organization, but there isn't a person alive who wouldn't prefer to feel that engaged every day. Can the two-dimensional business model really help you do this?

The professional dimension certainly *equips* a workforce to excel at their jobs, and the potential dimension provides employees with a *reason* to do well. But neither gives people any real *motivation* to put their heart and soul into their work.

What this system needs is a third, more personal dimension; one that goes deeper than a six-month evaluation or simple training module. It needs to connect people—not just through their vocations or capability, but through a genuine interest between employer and employees. This will create a shared desire to succeed and a unified definition of what success actually looks like.

Now, don't hear what we are not saying. Today's workforce is not inherently apathetic or lazy—after all—75% of an adult's waking hours are devoted to work. Take a second to think just how much time you spend getting ready for work, traveling to and from work, decompressing after work, or talking about your work—and that doesn't even include the time you actually spend working.

A person's job is also a defining facet of their identity. People talk about them to describe their social status, their lifestyle, and their character. For many, a job may even define their own perceived worth to society. Even further, a person's vocation is often the default question when first meeting them: "What do you do?"

Work is the first thing we ask our loved ones and spouses about when they return home: "How was your day?" It's often the first topic of discussion when catching up with a friend: "So how's work going?" These conversations show the central place our jobs have in our lives. So the notion of coming in to work and "leaving your personal life at the door" seems ridiculous when you compare the amount of time that we devote to work with how little time we truly spend away from it.

How we define ourselves and the lives we live are inseparable from the work we do. This makes it all the more difficult for the more than 70% of employees mentioned earlier that find their job unfulfilling or tedious. If we devote three out of every four waking hours of the day to work that leaves us feeling dissatisfied, how does that affect our families, our personal time, and the ways we bring value to our communities? Is it any wonder that most people would go to great lengths to find worth and fulfillment in their work and seek out an engaging work environment?

Practically speaking, it's true that everyone works for a wage first and any other benefits second. But in spite of the myth that all employees care about is a paycheck, the workforce today wants more than ever to work for objective-based businesses. That is, companies who value their employee's contributions toward a shared mission or goal.

IF YOUR EMPLOYEE ENGAGEMENT IS NOT CONFIDENTLY IN THE 80-90%+ RANGE, how much money is truly being lost through loss of productivity, attrition costs, customer and brand impact, etc.?

After all the time spent at work, shouldn't employees want to be invested in their company's cause? So why shouldn't a company want to be attached to its workers' interests?

To truly share in a common vision, companies must do more than offer occasional praise and opportunity for growth. The only way to engage your workforce is to invest in and show interest for their lives—you need to reciprocate the investment you'd like them to have. Employees want time to rest and recharge, the flexibility to live their lives, and an employer who cultivates a real relationship with them. Considering the time and mental commitment most people place in work, these are very reasonable requests.

It is in this third, personal dimension where most people feel their employers hold little interest. Employees don't feel valued because they aren't involved at a level deeper than their own tasks. Retention dwindles as people move from job to job, never finding a position they feel proud enough in to call a career. Business owners, therefore, find themselves spending more and more money on recruitment and benefits to entice new hires. And the idea of workplace loyalty begins to look like a relic of the past.

Loyalty among employees is no longer defined by what a worker will endure for the sake of a company. True loyalty can no longer be won through raises and promotions alone. Like any other meaningful relationship, workplace loyalty is circumstantial. It takes mutual respect and personal investment for employees to stay and feel a level of shared ownership in their company. After all, it takes that level of commitment in our friendships and marriages. The same must be true in a successful business relationship.

It is time for businesses to start Thinking 3D. Equip and outfit your workers as professionals. Recognize and reward their potential. But most importantly, invest in them personally.

A three-dimensional business model makes more sense because it helps workers to be engaged with their families, enjoy a more fulfilling life, and strive to be the best they can be for a company that truly values them as people. That is the new definition of success.

WHAT IS THE TRUE COST?

Whether or not companies and employees want to face the reality that is the true cost of an unengaged workforce, it still exists. We spend time and money doing regular check-ups to ensure all is well with our health, cars, and the financial details of our business. Why wouldn't we do the same health checkup on workforce engagement, since it has such an enormous impact on both our personal and professional lives?

To demonstrate the importance of investing in culture and the employer-employee relationship, let's look at a particularly telling analysis conducted by Gallup. For those that may not be familiar with Gallup, they provide companies with advice and analytics for a variety of organizational needs. One of their products—the Q12—is designed to measure employee engagement.

> "In 2012, Gallup conducted its eighth meta-analysis on the Q12 using 263 research studies across 192 organizations in 49 industries and 34 countries. Within each study, Gallup researchers statistically calculated the work-unit-level relationship between employee engagement and performance outcomes that the organization supplied. Researchers studied 49,928 work units, including nearly 1.4 million employees. This eighth iteration of the meta-analysis further confirmed the well-established connection between employee engagement and nine performance outcomes."[3]

---

[3] Sorenson, Susan. "How Employee Engagement Drives Growth." Gallup.com. Gallup, 20 June 2013. Web. 03 May 2016.

EMPLOYEE ENGAGEMENT AFFECTS KEY BUSINESS OUTCOMES

Work units in the top quartile in employee engagement outperform bottom-quartile units by 10% in customer ratings, 21% in productivity, and 22% in profitability. Work units in the top quartile also saw significantly lower absenteeism (37%), turnover (25% in high-turnover organizations, 65% in low-turnover organizations), and shrinkage (28%) and fewer safety incidents (48%), patient safety incidents (41%), and quality defects (41%).

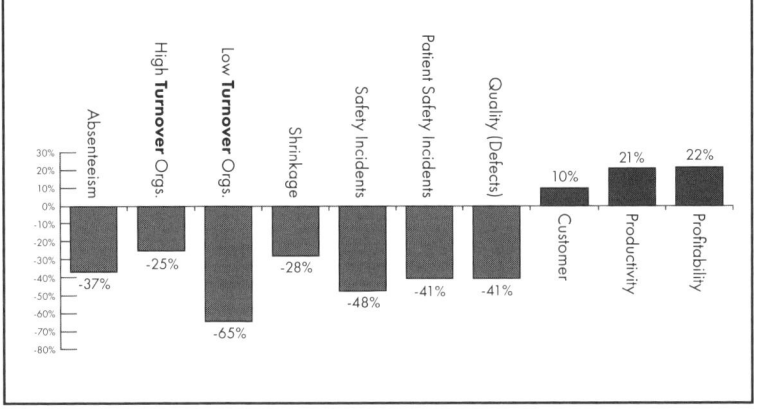

Absenteeism	-37%
High Turnover Orgs.	-25%
Low Turnover Orgs.	-65%
Shrinkage	-28%
Safety Incidents	-48%
Patient Safety Incidents	-41%
Quality (Defects)	-41%
Customer	10%
Productivity	21%
Profitability	22%

Source: GALLUP

MAXIMIZING THE POTENTIAL WITHIN THIS BOOK:

This book was designed to challenge you to pause and reflect on the topics that lie within these pages.

The quality of seed matters little to a farmer if they do not put the work in to prepare the soil, sow the seeds, water them, fertilize them, and cultivate the soil to ensure they get the maximum potential out of that seed. You are the farmer of your life. Because you've made the decision to invest your time into reading this book, why not ensure you are maximizing the full value of its potential? We invite you to journey with us to explore the power of true intention.

THINK 3D MOMENT:

Think about the last time you were successful at accomplishing something. Now consider:

1. What were your intentions going in?

2. What expectations did you have?

3. What level of energy, effort, and follow-through did you commit to in reaching your end result?

The principle of intention simply reveals that to accomplish anything of true significance, one must have real, concrete intention. The very fact that you have made the choice to open this book and read the first chapter says something about your inner desire to aspire for more and the belief that improvement is always possible.

One of the reasons most people or companies remain static in their environment is that the intention to change cannot come about when they do not even recognize that there is a problem. Mix the seeds of intent with the water of elevated thinking, add the sunlight of purposeful effort and it will always lead to change and growth. We welcome and congratulate you on taking the first step.

> "If you are not committed to helping cultivate and maximize the individual potential that lies within each of your employees holistically, then you cannot say you are fully committed to maximizing the full potential of your business."

THINKING 3D
Take-Away Thoughts

What are some of the ways your business or workspace can become more three-dimensional?

CHAPTER 2

SOMETHING TO BELIEVE IN

Imagine you are looking for a new job.

Maybe you're a recent college graduate, an overworked middle manager, or just someone seeking a better salary. Regardless of the initial motivating factor, you are truthfully searching for what everyone craves—a better life.

And this motivation shapes the criteria all prospective employees use to measure a company's attractiveness.

We are willing to wager that you've probably asked some variation of these same questions when considering a new job.

1. Is the salary enough to cover my expenses and allow me to live comfortably?
2. Will the typical workload place too much stress or mental strain on me?
3. Are the employees happy, motivated, and valued by their employer?
4. Will I be given enough scheduling flexibility and time off to spend with my family and for rest?

Now consider how effective or satisfied you would be in your current position if just one of those conditions wasn't met. These questions speak to our most basic needs, and are miles from unreasonable or selfish. They're quite the opposite, really—these criteria are the foundation on which an employee feels motivated to perform their best.

Now it's time to be honest.

Does your company offer the answers to these questions upfront during an interview? If it does, does it focus on any one in particular? What does your company advertise the most about itself to prospective employees?

For many people, the very first look into a business's motivations and inner workings takes on a familiar form: the mission statement.

Similar to the two-dimensional business model, a mission statement is both necessary and typical of most successful companies. It outlines a business's goals and purpose in the community. A mission statement can be anything from an exhaustive list of professional practices and ethics, to a simple, concise sentence. But a good mission statement confidently declares what a company does and who it serves.

However, like the two-dimensional model, a mission statement on its own leaves something to be desired. In the previous chapter, we discussed the time it takes for new employees to begin defining success on the same terms as their employers. The same is true with a mission statement.

It's difficult for any employee to get behind their company's cause if they haven't had the time to appreciate what they help the business accomplish. On top of this, they have had no say in their company's mission statement. They didn't help to write it. It isn't always an expression of their own goals. All entry-level employees have their own personal mission: make a good wage, work for good people, and live a good life.

So how do an employee's personal goals coincide with their company's goals? An employee may be on the same page with their organization's ethics, but in all honesty, that isn't the purpose of a mission statement.

This is not to imply mission statements are impractical or unnecessary. A successful business needs to set goals and have a clear direction. But it may be difficult for a new hire to identify with a company's cause, regardless of its good qualities.

Mission statements come up short in the same way the two dimensional business model does—they fail to *motivate* employees to join in their company's cause.

Many mission statements, especially those of non-profit institutions, include a set of beliefs or a code of ethics to inspire people to a greater cause than providing a product or service. But when used by a for-profit business, this union of belief and mission detracts from both, creating an unclear mismatch of ideals that's interpreted as contrived or indecisive. This is often the first hurdle when introducing the personal dimension into a business's culture: a disconnect between the purpose and the passion of a company.

The solution is simple: separate the two. To poise itself for success, a business needs both a mission statement *and* a belief statement.

This is not to be confused with a company's vision or the long-term change an organization wishes to effect. A belief statement is the passion behind the mission—it's what drives it.

For example, let's say a local contractor proudly displays their mission statement, "To serve homeowners and our community through quality craftsmanship and reasonable prices." It's certainly a noble cause and most people would have no problem working for a company like that. Now what if the owner went on to motivate his staff by declaring, "We believe the dream of owning a home should be a reality for everyone"?

How would you feel getting up each morning to work for that employer? How would you feel after each day?

"When employees belong, they will guarantee your success. And they won't be working hard for you and looking for innovative solutions for you, they will be doing it for themselves."

– Simon Sinek's, *Start with Why*

If a mission statement answers the question, "What does your company do?", then a belief statement should answer, "Why do you do it?"

Put another way, think of a company as a sailboat. If its mission statement acts as the sail, then its belief statement is the wind that fills the sail. In short, belief is the real power behind the mission.

So what powers your company? Why does it provide the products or services that it does, instead of others? These are questions whose answers can inspire employees to work for more than just a paycheck.

Employees today want to become ingrained in a business's culture. They want more than getting behind its products and revenue goals. People want to really invest in a space that encourages them to be whole, both professionally and in their personal lives. A solid belief statement is at the core of why people love what they do. If a company's beliefs resonate with its workforce, then so will its mission.

In Simon Sinek's book, "Start with Why", he says, "When employees belong, they will guarantee your success. And they won't be working hard for you and looking for innovative solutions for you, they will be doing it for themselves."

Take the United States Army Special Forces for example. Is it the assigned mission that makes this elite group so special? Or is it their beliefs and willingness to act upon them? Statements such as: "For God and country," "Leave no man behind," and even the Special Forces' own motto, "To liberate the oppressed" resonate a belief that inspires more than just service.

Much like a military slogan, a clear belief statement is a powerful recruitment tool. If a company is definitive in what it stands for, it can expect to hire people who want to work hard for them. Employees can expect to wake up feeling inspired and return home feeling fulfilled. Employers can help cultivate a community of people who not only work toward a common mission, but have a genuine desire to contribute.

Again, a belief cannot replace a solid mission statement. A company needs to have an identity and a goal just as much as a passion or a calling. A strong belief statement is a great first step for any business who wants to reconnect with their workforce, sow the seeds of real motivation, and inspire their employees' daily performance.

"One person with a belief is a social power equal to ninety-nine who have only interests.

– John Stuart Mill, English political philosopher and economist

THINKING 3D
Take-Away Thoughts
What would your belief statement be?

CHAPTER 3

ATTITUDE = ALTITUDE

Every business has several unique factors that add to its complexity. Many of these factors play a part in determining their culture. There is one factor, however, that applies universally no matter what line of business you are in, what you do, or who you are.

Attitude is a critical element that must be addressed before we can create a fulfilling and productive work environment. The attitude that people choose to wear each day is a foundational building block that directly impacts our perspective of everything else.

Our perspective is the lens through which we see the world. Failure to recognize the importance of attitude and perspective in the work place limits all subsequent action and well-intentioned efforts to build a great culture. On the other hand, a workforce with the right attitude is truly one without limits.

We've talked about ways to promote a healthy work culture. Inspiring employees to invest in their company can be as simple as separating the purpose and passion of the business. This is a great start to a fulfilling and productive work environment.

It's one thing to put down on paper what you think your business culture should look like. But it's another thing entirely to develop that culture.

A strong belief statement can make an employee feel good about the work they do. People feel inspired when they get behind their business's cause. It's time to start forging a real connection between the management and the workforce of your business.

But without any noticeable difference, how can these ideals become reality? With no change of pace, things are probably going to stay the same. Breathing new life into the entire culture of a workplace doesn't happen overnight.

Think of the oldest brand name you can. Maybe it's a pre-packaged food item from the turn of the century. Or it could be a family-owned business that's been the standard of quality for generations.

There's a reason these companies have lasted for as long as they have. Of course their foundations were built on a quality product or service, but their continued success can be pinned on one thing: recognizing and adapting to the need for change.

There isn't a business operating today that hasn't had to deal with change in some way, for better or for worse. But the most successful companies don't see change as just a necessity. They embrace it as a valuable commodity. Trends and technology change. Consumers' preferences, demands and expectations change. Why wouldn't we expect that our workplace culture would need to advance and change along with everything else?

This starts to speak to the power of the adaptive attitude of the leaders and employees within any organization. There are always going to be external factors that we simply cannot control. But in order to best position ourselves for whatever the future holds, having the right attitude is an absolute must if we're going to come out of the other side still standing and poised for success.

Overcoming obstacles and adapting to new trends is not just good business sense. Updating the workplace culture is crucial for any leader who wants employees to feel like a vital part of their company's future. And that makes everyone strive to give their best. This takes a personal investment of time and energy from employers and employees alike.

Think of it this way. When you speak with a financial advisor about retirement, the first thing discussed is how much money you will need to reach your goal. Only after that figure is set can you build a successful retirement plan. Once your plan is in place, you now have a goal in mind that will help keep your day to day grind in perspective. Your attitude now helps to align what you do with why you do it in order to reach your long term goal. All other decisions and strategies are based off that number.

To be successful in executing your plan, you'll need to stay the course of purposeful investments to get the desired return on that investment. Now take a moment to apply this thought to your daily actions. Are you making purposeful investments into your attitude regularly to give yourself the best chance to maximize gaining a return on the hours spent?

We should have the same mindset with our time and energy as we do with our financial investments. It requires a purposeful investment in yourself, your mind and your life to pay off in the form of a sound strategy for daily living.

Imagine a bucket of water next to a well. You can only fill your bucket once each morning and you spend each day deciding where best to pour your water. If the water represents all the time and energy you have every day, it's important to choose wisely. You will be faced with several opportunities for places you can choose to pour parts of your water into. However, some will be things you can't control and thus, it would be wasting water to put even a drop into that space.

So where do you pour your time and energy?

Of course there's our daily work. But there are many decisions we make at home that affect the rest of our day. Take a moment and evaluate how you begin each day. The first ten to fifteen minutes of your morning can set the tone for the rest of the day. Why not invest that time back into yourself? Breakfast with the family, a quiet moment reading a book, or a quick exercise may be the best way to start a great day. Choosing to be purposeful in the beginning of our day helps to "set" our mind in the direction we desire to go.

Now take this perspective into the next step of our day. When you enter into your workplace, do you have a purposeful intention of where and what you're going to pour your water into? In any work environment, we all face factors outside our control and influence. Yet we somehow allow ourselves to waste the precious commodity of time on concerns over which we have very limited control or influence. Ultimately, no amount of invested energy will return any benefits from this wasted time. Being purposeful in your intentions is now more important than ever.

This begins to explore the true freedom that the majority of people take for granted every day: the power of choice. In an unpredictable world where we are often limited in influencing the external circumstances, we can choose to control our attitude entering each new day. John C. Maxwell, best selling author and leadership guru, hit the nail on the head in stating that our "attitude is the prophet of our future."

"Attitude is the prophet of our future."

– John C. Maxwell

Let's revisit our bucket of water. After your work day is done, how much water is left in your bucket? Do you go home depleted of the energy necessary to fully engage in quality time with your family or other activities you enjoy? The lack of reflection in this space is what leads many people backwards in their actions and intentions. They'll say they work hard for their family or the activities they love to do outside of work, but will waste the time and energy meant for their loved ones and interests focusing on things they cannot control.

Purposefully choosing our attitude is a key factor in determining our outcome. To see the truth manifested here, simply study the life of anyone you would deem successful. What you're sure to find is a trail of intentional living, the right adaptive attitude toward their daily decisions, and the perspective that allows them to see through the appropriate lens guiding their path forward. Too often people are glamorized in the spotlight without the media telling the full story of the grind and determination it took for them to get there. Heavyweight boxing Champion Joe Frazier captured this best when he said, "Champions aren't made in the ring, they are merely recognized there."

This again highlights the power of perspective. The difficulties we face in our lives is the commonality we all share. How we view and respond to them is where we begin to see separation. Our attitude determines our perspective. Perspective influences decisions. Decisions influence actions. Actions influence outcomes.

We've already discussed just how much time and energy we devote to thinking about, preparing for, and working at our jobs. Where we devote our time and energy becomes more apparent while we're in the moment.

Our attitude determines our perspective.
Perspective influences decisions.
Decisions influence actions.
Actions influence outcomes.

People worry about their workloads, the way customers and coworkers treat them, getting time off or just getting through the day. These are things we sometimes have little influence, let alone control, over.

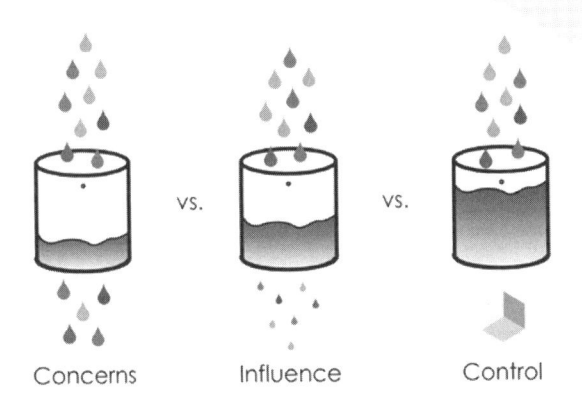

Concerns   vs.   Influence   vs.   Control

These areas certainly deserve concern and consideration. But of all the road blocks and obstacles you face each day at work, why would you pour your precious time and energy into things you can't even control?

Again, regardless of our external circumstances, there's only one thing you are always able to control: your attitude.

An attitude is really nothing more than the habits of a person's thought process. And, like any other kind of habit, you can learn or unlearn an attitude. All it takes is the repetition of a positive attitude to realize it as a good habit. Anthony Robbins, motivational speaker and self-help guru, says that repetition is the mother of skill. There is absolute truth in this statement. If we desire to have the best life possible at all levels, a great attitude is foundational to making this a reality.

On the opposite side of the coin, if you watch people who are negative, you begin to notice just how consistently they can be unhappy. Their future can be predicted with laser-like accuracy.

You know the folks we're talking about. These are the people who receive recognition at work and only respond with, "Well, it's about time." They complain about an inconvenience without trying to improve anything. They seem to have adopted the belief that it is the job of others to make them happy, and will not even entertain a shift in mindset to give themselves a chance at enjoying their life.

Negative people don't want to be a part of the culture of their workplace. They don't want to participate and don't want to be a part of a positive environment.

"Show me a culture where negative attitudes are allowed to remain and I'll show you a culture not maximizing its potential.

But the worst and most costly thing negative people do is bring down the entire workforce. They impact the engagement level of others, which in turn can have an effect on all the other factors within that person's job.

How many times have you seen a person diminished because of their positivity? At school, they're labeled a "teacher's pet." At work, they're called "brown-nosers." People who actually want to do their best and feel proud of their work are often marginalized by their unmotivated or uncaring peers.

A bad attitude is poisonous.

It takes far more positivity to counteract just one outspoken negative person. People who want more for themselves shouldn't be kept from acting on their goals for fear of being singled out. This is a toxic culture and the fact that many institutions allow these environments to exist is simply ridiculous, especially when truly trying to create a sustainable culture of success. Show me a culture where negative attitudes are allowed to remain and I'll show you a culture not maximizing its potential.

Negative attitudes are a huge obstacle for employees and employers alike and limit their true potentials. This is not to say one should never feel frustration at their job; we all feel constructive frustration at some point, but let us be clear about the difference. Criticism or feedback without positive intention quickly leads to negativity.

THINK 3D MOMENT:

Look at the life of Arnold Schwarzeneggar. His success can be directly attributed to attitude and perspective that he had. He overcame great odds just to get to the United States. He knew what he wanted and accepted no excuses in getting there. To say back in the 70s that an Austrian immigrant with a deep accent would become the world's best body builder, one of the highest grossing movie stars of all time, and the governor of California would have gotten anyone laughed at instantaneously. Fortunately for Arnold, he exercised his freedom to control his attitude regularly.

If you pay them –
   they'll do their job.
If you motivate them –
   they'll do what they need to do.
If you inspire them –
   they'll do what you need them to do.

The one true freedom within your control, and which is so influential in your life, is attitude. It has been pointed out by many that humans are the only species that don't strive to maximize their potential. Much of this starts with the failure to choose their attitude. Consequently, they succumb to the events of their life's experiences, settling for whatever hand was dealt to them.

While it's true that other people can affect the way we feel, we control how that reflects on our work and our attitude. Our attitude and perspective is an inside job. We control the filter in which we allow external factors to influence our reactions. Therefore, shouldn't we be intentional in how we allow life's input to affect our output?

We all face difficulties in life. But our attitude and how we choose to view and respond to life's difficulties remains the great separator. The real power we have is the choice of whether to let negativity determine who we are or to rise above it.

The reality is that if people don't care about the health of the business or the culture itself, they'll rarely care beyond the screen they're looking at, a to-do list, or going beyond the minimum they're required to do.

If you pay them – they'll do their job.
If you motivate them – they'll do what they need to do.
If you inspire them – they'll do what you need them to do.

With any business, the attitude sets the tone within the people and environment. The company's attitude towards their people will determine the potential they get out of them. The mentalities of "my way or the highway" and "employees should simply be happy to have a job" are fading away at the same rate as fax machines.

Attitude is the first step of the personal dimension.

Take stock where you spend your time and energy. It will help you face the day with a new perspective and a positive attitude. The attitude you carry to your coworkers and managers will affect the extent of everyone's potential.

ONE THING TO REMEMBER:

A positive attitude alone cannot fix a dysfunctional culture. Far too often businesses rely on the positive attitudes of their workforce to overcome a problem without ever actually addressing it. If you actually expect your workforce to only focus on that which they can control, they have to be confident that someone is focused on that which they cannot.

THINKING 3D
Take-Away Thoughts

What are some things you could do to more positively affect your attitude?

CHAPTER 4

THE
ECO-SYSTEM

Let's talk for a moment about bees.

These hard-working insects are a crucial part of the earth's ecosystem. Bees pollinate two-thirds of all the food we eat, and nearly 85% of all grown crops. These include most fruit and vegetables, nuts, cocoa beans, coffee, and tea. Crops grown as fodder for livestock are also pollinated by bees, as well as cotton and certain types of seeds used to produce oil.

Where would the human race be, along with many other species of animals, if bees no longer existed? It goes without saying that life as we know it would disappear. It's amazing how something as grand and critical as our planet's ecosystem can be delicate enough to hinge on the unseen daily work of bees.

A business ecosystem operates in much the same way.

Now most of us have held jobs considered to be "worker bee" positions. But this analogy is not trying to place more importance on one position over another. Every office and duty in a business ecosystem has value, and those workers in those positions must recognize their role. But too often, jobs seen as "low-level" or held by "front line workers" aren't appreciated enough.

All animals, including the humble bee, are born with an instinct for their purpose and role in their natural environment. We, on the other hand, need to discover where we fit into the grand scheme of things. When it comes to work environments, we are given a job description.

Nearly every species of bird relies on bees to pollinate seed-bearing plants for their survival. People also need to recognize those who sustain their own roles.

An employee's contribution to their ecosystem isn't just a completed to-do list. This is knowledge that must be shared with a passion between all employees.

To shrug and say "accountants do accounting" and "sales people do sales" is no longer good enough. We all need an understanding of how these departments feed into each other. What one employee does every day at their desk doesn't affect them alone. It helps every other person in every branch do their work and vice versa.

Does the natural world separate itself into zones based on each species' role in the ecosystem? Imagine how ridiculous a forest would look this way, not to mention how badly it would operate.

Grass, flowers, and trees aren't clumped into groups. Animals aren't isolated based on their eating habits. Nature doesn't work in boxes, so why should we?

Knowing what you do and who you impact is such a basic thing for an employee to understand. Yet this is a major part of the personal dimension. Making this one small change to a business's ecosystem can have a huge impact on employees.

This speaks to the power of a unified culture, purposely created for the purpose of moving towards a common goal that is influenced by a shared belief statement.

Knowing who depends on you and who you depend on in return is such a powerful contribution to job satisfaction. That peace of mind impacts home life in a positive way which, in turn, affects how an employee returns to their job each day. This begins to highlight the reciprocating effect of work-life balance.

Seemingly, however, the direction of the workforce appears to be leaning toward individualism becoming the ultimate goal that most strive for in this country. Community has taken a backseat to being your own person with your own ideals. Unfortunately, this mentality shift has affected the workplace system. People are less likely to identify themselves by what they contribute, content to keeping their heads down and simply putting in the hours each day. It highlights the difference between when asked by a family member or friend what they do and their reply being, "I just take phone calls," versus, "I get to help resolve customers concerns."

Even with the impact that our jobs truly do have on our lives, with us spending close to 75% of our waking hours with work on our mind, most people never stop and acknowledge it. Instead, they simply deal with it as their accepted lot in life until their dissatisfaction pushes them to look for greener pastures.

Is it any wonder people no longer stay with a company their entire careers?

There's no use denying it any longer. The life-long employee model from previous generations is no longer functional. It doesn't work personally or financially. With job retention at an all-time low, it's starting to cost employers more and more to hire new workers.

WHAT IS THE COST of attrition for your company? When thin margins can be the difference between whether you're in the red or in the black, this often unrealized true cost can be the difference in swinging the pendulum.

On average, studies have shown that the cost to replace an employee can be anywhere from 16-21% or higher of that person's yearly wage.[4] That means even entry-level positions starting with a $25,000 salary cost around $5,000 just to rehire. These figures speak to the bottom line cost of replacement. It doesn't include the ripple effect that it has on limiting a business's ability to build a culture if there is difficulty in keeping tenured people around to help maintain the momentum needed to truly progress.

We understand many businesses operate on thin margins. That's why it's puzzling to hear excuses why companies can't justify the time and cost of changing their workplace culture. It's understandable that with the marketplace moving at the speed it is, with increasing competition and regulations, or a variety of other day-to-day requirements to run a successful business, how looking at building a successful culture seems to move to the bottom of prioritization. However, if we ask ourselves whether or not we're positioning ourselves for long-term success through a positive and sustainable culture, what's our honest answer? At this point, businesses can't afford not to change.

And it isn't just the cost of rehiring that's at stake here. Without a fulfilling culture to work in, employees are using their jobs as a means to an end. They aren't feeling satisfied, which leads to a lowered average of them utilizing their potential. When people work for a paycheck, they aren't doing their best. A company with that kind of workforce isn't going to be as successful as it could be.

[4] Merhar, Christina. "Employee Retention - The Real Cost of Losing an Employee." Zanebenefits.com. Zane Benefits, 4 Feb. 2016. Web. 03 May 2016.

So how can employers balance caring for their company's success and its workforce?

It comes down to the employee's investment in their company. What reason have they received to share in the business's mission? What is their stake in all this? Do they have a clear path to personal success? Are they obtaining a good standard of living by investing themselves?

Whether businesses want to come to grips with it or not, the hard and fast reality is that the working mentality that employees "should just be happy to have a job" is fast retiring, along with the generation it was a part of.

When leaders pay attention to caring for their employees, they will return the favor. Job satisfaction, loyalty, and higher productivity doesn't just happen. Employers have to show their workers the impact their jobs have on them and on each other.

Think about it for a moment. Going back to the mid-20th century, in an era coming off of the great depression and unemployment rates around 25%, simply having a good job that promised a path to the "American Dream" was good enough to drive a successful culture. Employees knew that if they came to work, worked hard, they would be promised a steady income and a pension in which they'd be able to provide for their family and have a secure future. Simply having a good job was enough to fuel their tank of engagement.

Fast forward to today. With unemployment rates at a fraction of that from a half century ago, more options than ever in terms of career choices, and a shifting of what defines the "American Dream," what promise does a company give to its employees that would inspire them to stay with them for life? The average working individual will log more than 100,000 hours at work in their lifetime. Simply providing a steady job is far from enticing enough to create a successful culture today.

The need to revolutionize workplace culture is increasingly becoming more evident. Unfortunately, far too many companies are slow in adoption. This is often due to it being easier to continue down the path of the familiar rather than being bold in setting out into unknown territory.

This undeniable shift can be likened to the times of Henry Ford. If businesses were asked in the early 20th century what they needed, they most likely would have said faster horses. The lack of adapting to a change in the times greatly benefited business owners such as Ford tremendously. While the majority of companies kept on with business as usual, he identified an opportunity to transform how things have always been done. He recognized that the production line would help lead to what could be called the Model T revolution, transforming a new way of doing business.

Similarly to a hundred years ago, many companies are failing to recognize this growing paradigm shift in the workplace environment. Consequently, they aren't taking steps to build a "Model T" revolutionary culture within their businesses. The failure to adapt can and will leave many companies in the similar positions of other businesses from that time very few have ever heard of because they no longer exist.

Workplace culture is either something you invest in or something you will pay for.

Think about how many hours of each day an employee sees their spouse or children versus their coworkers. It's an unavoidable way of life. The people we love most are the ones we interact with the least. This reality is a basic commonality that every working individual shares. Therefore, the same advantages of creating a positive culture are universally beneficial to everyone.

We may not be able to change the imbalance of time spent at work versus home. But people can change the relationships they have with their coworkers and the atmosphere in which they spend at work each day. Companies can evolve what engagement means to them and their employees. We can all shift our paradigm of how we view investing time, energy and effort into our attitudes towards how we spend our time at work.

In all honesty, what do you know about the people at your job? What do you *really* know? A favorite sports team or maybe a hobby? How much of what we say to our coworkers actually means something? Do we ask how they're doing out of habit and courtesy or do we have a genuine interest in their lives?

Sure, you're probably not going to become best friends with everyone at the office. But if you're invested in your business's ecosystem then you have a shared value with everyone else there. As much time as people spend with each other at work, it's absurd not to invest in things that truly add value to our lives.

Know your role in the ecosystem, appreciate other peoples' contributions, and connect with your coworkers on a personal level. These are great things for a business to strive to have. The problem companies have in adopting these ideas stem from a simple fact:

You cannot measure happiness.

Sales do not equal employee engagement. Productivity does not equal a positive attitude. Focusing on numbers and hoping they motivate people is not reality. This can be scary for a lot of employers, especially if they're used to measuring success in this way. But using success to fuel engagement is really putting the cart before the horse.

An unattended culture will always become an unintended culture.

Challenge yourself to go beneath the surface and into the meaning behind our everyday actions and words to get a glimpse of more truth about our culture than most pay attention to.

Pause for a moment and walk through what this shift could mean to your life and to the lives of those you work with every day. Challenge the myth of culture in a box where we are asked to settle for the environment we spend such an enormous amount of time in.

WHAT'S THE TRUE LEVEL OF ENGAGEMENT IN YOUR WORK CULTURE?

Culture challenge – The observation test:

On a Friday afternoon, sit in your car unnoticeably in the parking lot. What do the body language and expressions of people leaving for the weekend say? Potentially:

- "I survived another week"
- "Finally I'm out of there"

What kinds of dialogue do you hear floating in the atmosphere on a regular basis? To the simple passing question "How are you doing?" would you frequently hear:

- "It's Monday" (In a Eeyore voice) – Sigh, another week
- "It's almost the weekend" – I can't wait to get out of here
- "Not bad" – so not good
- "It's almost Friday" – I'm not fully engaged in the now, as I can't wait for a day not even here yet

Imagine if your workplace was one that you and your coworkers came into work inspired and went home satisfied. How would that change your mood and attitude going home? Would that change the mental engagement you were able to spend towards the activities you do outside of work? Would that allow you to enjoy your entire weekend and not waste half of your Sunday dreading having to rinse and repeat the current work cycle of life? Why isn't it possible?

Now let's reengage wherever you're at in your current state. The reality of culture is that it's like a huge cruise ship. It takes a long time to build and is hard to change direction once it's going full speed. But it can be done. It does, however, take very purposeful and consistent effort to change the direction you want to go. That little rudder is the small part responsible for sending the signal to steer the huge vessel towards its new destination.

In the same way, it takes a small but specific and intentional shift, to steer a culture in a new direction.

A great culture doesn't happen by chance. A great culture doesn't come easy. What could you be losing by not maximizing the potential of a great culture? How much energy do you have left in your tank when you go home at night? When most of us say we work hard for our families, do our families by default get the leftovers from the result of long, energy-draining days?

We admit this is a bold idea. It will take intentional effort to realize where your business is headed. It will take honesty to face the reality that things need to change. Permanent changes take time, energy, and an effort to care for worker bees.

THINKING 3D
Take-Away Thoughts
How would a Think 3D culture affect the way that you work and/or live?

CHAPTER 5

AFTER YOU!

What does a good leader look like?

Much like a successful business, a good leader is such a vague idea. But everyone knows one when they see one or work for one.

Competent leadership isn't just crucial for a healthy workplace culture. It's universal across all aspects of life. People know who they want to follow and they feel inspired to do so.

But where do good leaders come from?

Would anyone be able to rise to leadership with a big enough raise to motivate them? Should employers just expect natural leaders to fall into higher positions? Or should people be raised up through guided preparation and coaching?

It might be easier to answer what a leader is *not*.

1. LEADERS AREN'T MADE WITH PROMOTIONS.

As we've discussed in earlier chapters, employees want to work for more than just a paycheck. If more money can't make people happy or more engaged at their jobs, why would it make someone a better leader?

A promotion on Friday and a few hours of training the next Monday is no way to prepare someone to lead. For many companies, promotions to a leadership role often come from a pool of employees who do great work in their current position. Being effective in your current role doesn't automatically prepare anyone to lead others. Unfortunately, this is often the extent of the criteria considered without any additional investment to help prepare people for that next level. People should be equipped to lead, not pushed.

A good leader should take stock of the tools given them to do their jobs effectively. Naturally learning good leadership in most trades often takes years of trial and error. A leader required to grow into their position will result in missed opportunities and directly impact employees with the gap in the leader's current competency. So it is well worth it for businesses to invest months of training into apprentice leaders to help accelerate this process as much as possible. Throwing them to the wolves is not a great strategy when the downstream impacts can be extensive.

THINK ABOUT the time, energy, and effort spent to train people to do certain jobs. Take a plumber as an example. The hours spent learning the trade are extensive because it is critical to the effectiveness of them doing their job well. If there is a failure to properly train them, or aspects of learning their craft are skipped over, the results can be disastrous and costly when they attempt to do functions critical to their job. No one would think that simply because someone excelled at delivering parts and had great knowledge of the general process, they would be able to handle the next level without the necessary training.

In that example, we're discussing an individual contributor role. When we shift to consider a leadership position, how much more critical is it that we should train someone that will have impact and influence over several people? The effectiveness of their leadership capabilities can exponentially benefit or hinder the people they lead. Isn't the investment worth it?

2. LEADERS DON'T EXPECT PEOPLE TO JUST FOLLOW BECAUSE.

As we've discussed, a title does not make people into a leader. A good leader takes time to step outside of themselves and ask, "Why should people follow me?" Because many so-called leaders fail to reflect on this question, they are simply taking a walk. Without willing followers, you cannot "lead" people anywhere.

The "do what I say just because" mentality is never a good reason to follow anyone. Sure people may have to follow suit due to position or authority, but it'll be a "check the box" minimum effort to do the basic amount required and no one will be happy about it.

Good leadership shows people *why* they should follow. They also help employees see the WIIFM (what's in it for me). When people see and understand the why, and believe that their leader genuinely cares about them beyond simple subordinate relationships, they'll willingly give them their extra effort to go beyond the basic requirements of the job.

3. LEADERS DON'T ALWAYS HAVE TO BE MANAGERS.

Being a leader doesn't require subordinates. Any employee at any level can be a leader within their work space, their communities, and their own lives. It's people like this who make the best leaders, even if their job title doesn't reflect it. John C. Maxwell, best selling author and leadership guru, says that leadership is *influence*. Any employee with influence, whether with a coworker, direct report, or senior leadership, has the ability to be a leader.

A true leader recognizes who they are, understanding their role in the business ecosystem as well as their coworkers' roles. Only then can leaders foster the shared mission of the company. A good leader also understands that the personal and professional places their coworkers come from are all different. They recognize and appreciate the various personalities within those around them and seek to see the best in everyone, instead of allowing differences to be a separating factor. They know how to use the personal dimension to lead everyone to a common goal.

4. LEADERS AREN'T BLIND TO THE POWER OF THEIR ACTIONS.

Regardless of position or title, when you have influence, people will see you as a leader in some capacity. It has been said that people can't hear what you're saying over what you're doing.

Monkey see – monkey do. How will your actions impact those who follow you?

Whether it is fair or not, we're always teaching others about who we are. What you're teaching them is up to you. Given this, what are others truly taking from the example you set forth? We all know that with actions speaking louder than words, respect is hard to gain and can be lost in a moment.

One major fallacy that plagues the assumptions of many leaders is that "people should just get it." The reality, however, is that each person has been uniquely shaped by a lifetime of experiences that only they went through. Holding people to an expectation of "just knowing" is a dangerous cliff to be standing on. True, there are a lot of things that most people would deem common sense, however, we all have things about ourselves that someone, somewhere may think are contrary to what they would consider common sense.

The importance of the impact and influence of our actions speaks to the power behind the principle of exposure. The principle of exposure simply states that what we are consistently exposed to has the power to influence who we become. A good leader takes into account the downstream impacts of their decisions and actions. They are deliberate in their interactions, knowing their influence can and will go beyond the effect they have on themselves.

Great leaders clearly understand the imperative nature of exposing those around them to higher levels of thinking and belief. Faith is the focus of the mind's eye. Leaders help their people see the power of what is possible by instilling faith into their core belief.

5. LEADERS AREN'T EXEMPT FROM HELP.

Another huge fallacy people have about leaders is they should "just know" what their bosses want from them. Employers may feel that an employee promoted to a leadership position should inherently know what to do without being told. This is a very unrealistic expectation.

This is like saying that once we get married we should "just know" how to act as a spouse; or once we have a child we should "just know" how to be a parent. We all know how well that works out. The best path forward for any newly married couple or a new parent is learning from those who have already successfully navigated that path. Their shared knowledge and experience is invaluable in helping to accelerate the process of developing successfully into these new roles.

Unfortunately, the expectation that a leader should "just know" often also comes from those they will lead; that somehow a leadership 101 course was automatically downloaded into their brain when they were promoted to their leadership position. Leadership, like almost everything else, is learned from experience and training.

Leaders need a personal investment from their superiors as much as they need to invest in their own team.

Companies rarely come alongside their managers and supervisors to make sure they're doing well at home and in their work. Dismissing the idea that someone in a leadership role would need any help simply because "they're leaders" is a fatal mistake in a business ecosystem.

WHAT IS YOUR LEADERSHIP EFFECTIVENESS COSTING YOU?

What percentage would you give your current leadership effectiveness in your organization?

Let's use the example of a simple 3-tier leadership model.

- Leader A leads 4 leaders at level B.
- Leaders at level B lead 10 people each at level C.

If Leader A has a leadership effectiveness of 80%, 20% of the potential effectiveness of developing the leaders at level B is lost.

In turn, if leaders at Level B started out with a leadership effectiveness of 70%, and are being shorted 20% in the development they're getting because of the leadership effectiveness gap of their boss, how does that roll down to level C?

Think about what happens when a stressed and overworked leader is expected to motivate their team. If that leader isn't giving their best effort, how can they be expected to inspire others to give theirs?

Think of the effects this can have on a workplace's culture. This kind of situation practically breeds negative attitudes.

When you couple this thought with the number of people each given leader throughout your organization has direct responsibility and influence over, it is plain to see how much potential opportunity is wasted if leadership development isn't purposefully a part of the strategy.

But checking in on leaders isn't just an employer's job. Leaders at every level within a team can help bridge this gap, investing in their own managers on a personal level. In an ideal workplace, personal investment would travel upward and downward. Intentionally applying this is a key foundational piece of a good leader.

6. LEADERS CAN'T SEE EVERYTHING.

Imagine you and a search party have to find a lost item in an overgrown field. How would you arrange this group? You probably wouldn't march everyone through the grass single-file. Not only would this method be a huge waste of time, but everyone would be scanning the same area without talking to each other.

As ridiculous as that sounds, this is how a lot of teams function. One person leads the way and everyone else falls in line. This may get the work done, but how much more effective would it be to include many perspectives on a shared goal?

When leaders walk alongside people, the mission is shared among the entire team.

There's a reason search parties fan out and communicate with each other. Every member knows their role and supports the people next to them. The organizer multiplies the effectiveness of the task by working alongside his team. The work is transformed from a job that has to get done into a goal that inspires people to contribute.

If companies are always looking for the best way to do business, why wouldn't they use all the eyes they have at their disposal? If you don't want to continually see the same things, you will always need new perspectives.

Some of the most successful companies have multiple avenues to encourage their employees of all levels to be involved in providing feedback and/or input on a regular basis. Companies that do not have missed a huge opportunity as front-line employees often recognize ways to improve or identify risk.

If you've ever watched the television show Undercover Boss, have you ever seen an episode where the boss didn't end up improving something that came from hearing and seeing the operations side of the business directly from their front-line team members? Multiple pairs of eyes and perspectives are always better than a singular point of view.

7. EVERYONE CAN'T ALWAYS BE THE LEADER.

Leadership is something that should evolve throughout a business. But raising up a leader is usually based on when a company needs the position filled. An employee is rarely promoted on the spot when they prove themselves to be a true leader.

It's all about timing.

Every employee is capable of becoming a leader in every aspect of their lives. A business that understands this and expects it in their workforce hires people who prepare themselves to become leaders one day. John Wooden, the iconic UCLA basketball coach and leadership guru, said, "When opportunity comes, it's too late to prepare."

> "When opportunity comes, it's too late to prepare"
> – John Wooden

Unfortunately, many people have a shortsighted vision of development. They have adopted a mindset of "give me the position and I'll show you what I can do." Demonstrating leadership ahead of getting the position says, "I'll show you what I can do, then I'll get the position".

Everyone has natural talent in different areas, both for leading and for inspiring leadership in others. But you can't give to people what you don't have yourself.

This is important to understand when you find yourself in a leadership position or when working in a team under a leader. To believe in yourself and your role, you must know where you are in an ecosystem and what you have to contribute.

"Most people don't lead their lives; they just accept them."

– John C. Maxwell

You can't get a return on an investment you don't make. You are your greatest asset, invest like it.

When you appreciate your own strengths and weaknesses, you are able to pass that positivity on to your teammates. Without leaders and coworkers, it becomes much harder to realize your full potential. Likewise, your strengths strengthen others around you.

You can't get a return on an investment you don't make. You are your greatest asset, invest like it. Why wouldn't you be intentional about maximizing the potential that may be lying dormant within, just waiting to be watered and nurtured? Unfortunately, most people spend more time planning their retirement than improving their personal potential, which will in turn have the greatest impact on their retirement.

All this feeds into the workplace ecosystem and leads back to that company's belief statement. Every employee in your business's culture excels at something. A true leader believes in themselves and in their team. They have the ability to be a catalyst to lead people forward because they have belief and confidence in themselves and consistently instill this same belief and confidence into others.

Most of all, a good leader promotes a willingness to participate, works alongside their team, and shows them the path to a fulfilling career.

Leadership is both one of the most overused terms, and underappreciated effectiveness tools in most companies. Due to the nature of a business's line of work, the skill set of their workforce, and many other factors, there is no one-size-fits-all leadership development model. This does not, however, give an excuse for every company not to have a leadership development strategy. Overall, leadership qualities are universal, and the foundational principles of an effective leader spread far beyond the tasks of any particular line of business.

THINKING 3D
Take-Away Thoughts

List 10 traits of an ideal leader:

(How many do you possess?)

CHAPTER 6

DO YOU SEE WHAT I SEE?

In chapter two, we talked about what it means for a company to have a vision. Businesses may attempt to interchange the phrases "vision statement" and "belief statement." And while they may look similar at first glance, these tools are used in very different ways.

As we discussed, a company's belief statement is what drives the business. It represents the passion that motivates a higher calling than just a product or service.

If a mission statement answers the question "What do we do?", then the belief statement answers "Why do we do it?"

But these are questions usually asked by customers or investors. Clients and employees can both get behind a good belief. But a company's vision needs to focus more on internal affairs.

Going back to our nautical analogy, a company's ship raises a solid mission statement which acts as the sail. And the wind of a noble belief statement fills that sail with purpose. But it's the rudder, or the company's vision, that actually steers the vessel.

The vision of a company cannot be some lofty dream in the sky. It has to be a fact in progress. A vision is a business saying to its employees, "This is where we're headed and we *will* get there." It's the end goal, the reward for investing in the belief.

A vision must be clear, genuine, and common knowledge to all levels of employment. Employees operating under a good vision can see how what they're doing ties into helping the company and more importantly for themselves personally.

Take, for example, our scenario with the contractor business. If you'll remember, the mission statement read: "To serve homeowners and our community through quality craftsmanship and reasonable prices."

The business went on to inspire their staff with this belief statement: "We believe the dream of owning a home should be a reality for everyone."

Who wouldn't want to get up every day to go to work for that company? Who wouldn't feel motivated to put their heart and soul into their work?

Let's be honest. That inspiration would probably wear off in a few days for most people. Of course, a reminder of a company's beliefs now and then can reignite the passion for the work you do.

But a daily vision that actually *shows* where your work is guiding the company is something that lasts.

Here's an example of what that contractor's vision might look like:

> "From each foundation poured to every roof shingled, we deliver our customer's goals."

This is what should be seen printed next to every desk and in every construction vehicle this contractor owns. This vision is the clear, undiluted purpose of each employee's daily work. Every person working at this company now understands that their goals are the client's goals.

"Leaders are leaders because they communicate effectively and frequently. They're continually communicating the organization's mission, the benchmarks of the goals, and the casting of the vision."

– Steve Durkac, *21 Motivational Insights on Leadership Enrichment*

A vision needs to be *visual*. Every employee needs to see tangible results that connect them and their work to the shared mission. Is there clarity in the vision of how the efforts each person makes on a regular basis helps to continue blowing wind into the sail of the business? Is the vision applicable and simple so that everyone easily understands it?

A successful vision flows down through a business like water into the soil. It cannot skip layers along the way. A vision should be shared passionately by the leaders throughout the organization to the point that it is contagious.

When communicating the vision, is it shared in a way that everyone at every level can connect to it? Where they can share in the belief and see themselves partaking in the mission to reach the vision?

Above all, a vision must be something an employee can own. It has to be real to them in order for it to truly be effective. People want to feel and be a part of something great. They want to feel empowered, valued, and understood. When these things happen, they will fully embrace the vision.

"Success is entirely achievable if you start by crystallizing to your mind the key goals in life that you are passionate about or that move you or set you alight or float your boat or, to put it another way, if you don't tell the taxi driver where to take you, he can't get you there."

– Sue Stevenson

Once an employee understands their role in the ecosystem, personal responsibility begins to take root. Duty to a job creates pride in the work. And when you're proud of the work you do, you're going to put your heart and soul into that job.

THE PRINCIPLE OF EXPOSURE

> The Ritz-Carlton model. The vision is apparent throughout the company from CEO to bellman. Because the vision is shared consistently and every employee is exposed to it regularly, it helps put the wind in the sails of where the company wants to go.

This is where the personal dimension really takes shape.

It isn't a product that's going to inspire people to come to work each day. It's what that product achieves that gives employees a stake in the mission. Show people the impact they make every day, and you'll make an impact that can't be measured with quarterly reports.

THINKING 3D
Take-Away Thoughts
What is your vision?

CHAPTER 7

...BUT CAN YOU DO IT AGAIN?

B elief, vision, attitude, leadership, and the ecosystem of our work place: these are the tools of the personal dimension.

Thinking 3D creates a culture where everybody is speaking the same language. It's a mindset that finally allows every level of a business to start to understand the other. Every employee is in a position to progress and show leadership. Everyone has an investment in the people around them and works side by side on equal ground.

But that's the finish line. How do you start?

These are extraordinary ideas. It's a lot to take in. Yes, this will take time. And yes, it will cost money. That's what any good investment requires. But the most difficult part of leading this journey is how lonely things are going to feel at first.

To be extraordinary is to be lonely.

Anything less would just be ordinary. Knowing this, it's important to share Thinking 3D with other like-minded people around you. This will of course give your idea traction down the road. But it also gives you a group to draw upon when you experience resistance to change.

Taking on this business model is something other people may not want to do. A leader can expect to get pushback, but recognize that this is normal.

It's okay for people to be skeptical at first.

Remember that most people today grow up learning not to take everything they are told at face value. It's an unfortunate side effect of the freedom of being an individual. People are scared of being scammed. They take new ideas with a grain of salt. They've been suckered in the past and the experience has left them cynical.

Not only that, but the idea of investing in your coworkers and adopting your company's beliefs will be uncomfortable to some people. There is a mentality that lies deep within many employees that says a job is for working, not connecting with people. Work is a means to an end, not an opportunity for growth.

Have you thought about your strategy to get past this?

Thinking 3D isn't another "flavor of the month" initiative that fizzles out once everyone rolls their eyes and goes through the motions. Just like implementing a vision, the entire personal dimension needs to be reinforced daily by example.

How effective would it be for an employer to tell the entire workforce at once, "Okay, people. This is how we do business from now on"? Just imagining a superior telling you that should give you a knee-jerk reaction to resist.

In order to introduce Thinking 3D, leaders cannot only adopt the personal dimension for themselves. If the goal is encouraging employees to replicate and own these ideas, they must see this every single day. They must be immersed in it.

Repetition is the key to replication.

Imagine hanging out with a group of your friends. If you've known these people for a long time, the group dynamic is probably pretty balanced. Everyone in this circle knows how to act and react to each other. There's an unspoken unity that defines what kind of jokes you tell, the topics brought up, and the social role of each person.

Now imagine one of your friends has brought along their new boyfriend or girlfriend.

Changes the group dynamic a bit, doesn't it? If this has happened to you before, you know how fast people adjust to compensate for a change like this. Manners are suddenly better, conversation shifts to more universal topics, and inside jokes are kept to a minimum. All this change without a word spoken to announce it.

Also, when someone new joins an established group, there's always that feeling of instant resistance. Even if nothing is known about this new person, their immediate reaction is an innate desire for things to go back to the way they were.

In time, even most strangers can become friends. It's only through repetition that acceptance comes naturally. All it needs is intentional exposure from one person.

Allow coworkers to resist change and discover for themselves how Thinking 3D benefits them. It may sound counterintuitive, but sometimes employees will resist adopting a better ecosystem—even if it improves their overall quality of life. Again, this speaks to people's natural instincts to resist change. You're not simply facing the task of getting people to adapt to the logic of Thinking 3D, you're up against the sum of each employee's lifelong habits and beliefs. Habits and beliefs formed from thousands of experiences over their lifetimes.

If employees are exposed to a vision of fulfilling and meaningful work, they will own that idea and replicate that exposure to their peers. To drive home the power behind the simple principle of exposure, imagine you've relocated to London for two years. Simply by mere exposure, you'll naturally begin to adopt parts of the English culture. Some of your language and vernacular will change. Some of your mannerisms will shift. None by intention, but simply through mere exposure.

REWIND TIME TO TWENTY YEARS AGO.

Imagine convincing companies that a culture like Zappos or Google would – or should – ever work. You would have been laughed out of the room. Or imagine a few decades prior to that when a gentleman named Steve from Silicon Valley was selling a vision of what personal computers would do to change the world. Today these few examples seem obvious. However, because they were radical ideas beyond what the majority knew, these concepts seemed inconceivable to the majority at the time because they were radical ideas that challenged the status quo.

The good news for those who dare to see the truth in where trends are going are the ones who benefit from being ahead of change. They become the minority of believers who implement first and innovate. History has left plenty of examples of ordinary people who simply made the decision to put forth the extra, and their outcomes led to extraordinary results.

HOW INTENTIONAL ARE YOU ABOUT WHAT YOU'RE ALLOWING YOURSELF TO BE EXPOSED TO?

Without intention, we allow ourselves to be exposed to wasteful information that the media regularly bombards us with.

Ultimately then, we should say that we're intentionally not growing. Choose to purposefully invest in yourself and control what you allow yourself to be exposed to. Refuse to be trapped by the mediocrity of what has always been. Unless you're okay with saying aloud, "I'm satisfied with being average", then it will take the extra beyond the ordinary to tap into the possibility of greatness.

Creating this type of ecosystem within any business will reap exponential benefits. Instilling cultural replication into any business is the critical part of sustaining this environment of long-term success. A few key questions to focus on asking are:

1. Can you do it again?
2. Can you do it consistently?
3. Do we have the determination to overcome the resistance and obstacles that will come?

"Routines without ongoing assessment lead to stagnation and mediocrity. Most individuals, teams, and organizations rise to a challenge or fall to the familiar."

– T.D. Jakes, Author and Pastor

Author and entrepreneur Michael Gerber, whom Inc. Magazine called "the World's #1 Small Business Guru," says, "Systems permit ordinary people to achieve extraordinary results predictably." Of course, like anything worthwhile, this takes an upfront cost of time, money, energy, and effort. The real question behind this is, can anyone really afford not to invest in their ecosystem?

Most companies have good intentions and have likely already taken several steps toward improving their business in the past. Deep down, they know the value of what this could do for their business and their employees. Where obstacles are often met is in the space of replication. Creating a culture where the task at hand is everyone's responsibility requires a paradigm shift.

We've all been taught through years of school how to learn. Very few are ever asked to learn so they can be able to teach and replicate what they've learned to others. The mindset of learning to teach takes on a whole different level of intent than when you go into something to learn yourself. However, when we focus on something with that intent, it becomes clearer than we ever thought possible because our brains are now wired to pull out the necessary things needed to replicate.

Remember the principle of exposure? What we are consistently exposed to has the power to influence who we become. It is extremely easy to fall back to the norm of old habits and the well-worn grooves of our normal thought processes. Breaking the mold of mediocrity takes purposefulness, and when we change our routines and habits on purpose, our future outlook begins to change.

WHAT IS YOUR COMPANY'S STRATEGY AROUND DEVELOPING ITS PEOPLE POTENTIAL?

With employees' salaries being one of the largest — if not the largest — expenses for most businesses, why would any employer not invest to maximize the return on this fixed cost? Would a farmer pay top dollar for a calf from a prize bull and then not intentionally develop that calf to maximize the investment tenfold of what he paid? Many companies have programs in place that work to develop their top-tier talent. But even if those programs target the top 20%, what is being left on the table with the other 80%?

> "**Motivation** is not permanent, but neither is bathing. However, if we bathe every day, we are ahead of the game. From a motivational point of view, if we deliberately seek encouragement (motivation) on a daily basis, it will become a habit and enable us to get ahead and stay ahead in life."
>
> – Zig Ziglar, Author and motivational speaker

Unfortunately, most people never give this any real thought and thus place little value on it. Without purposeful exposure, the average person only grows in small increments or at the rate of inflation by accident. To achieve any growth beyond this, it is necessary to consistently invest time and energy into planting the seeds that will benefit our future.

Gathering the momentum to build a lasting and successful culture takes more than simple motivation. Motivation gets millions off their couch on January 1st every year, but without a lasting change to daily habits and actions, the vast majority fall back to the mediocrity of familiarity. To make change truly stick, there needs to be on-going, continuous, and purposeful intent. Again, change takes time. At times it may seem like chipping away at a concrete wall with a butter knife. But word-of-mouth has real power to spread ideas. Allow employees to talk to each other and the personal dimension will begin to set down roots.

But the real reward for encouraging a workforce to Think 3D is what people take home to their families. Replication really thrives when an employee goes home energized and wakes up inspired. This idea is not just about making a business more productive and successful. Thinking 3D is about creating a sustainable culture where employees can see a pathway to success for themselves, a pathway that in turn fuels the success of the company.

This begins to spill over into their personal lives. They begin to not simply see a job as a means to an end, but an engrafted part of who they are. Once we begin to see this type of work-life experience, we become encouraged that a richer, more satisfying life is possible. Thinking 3D is about making people happier.

The good news is, it's never too late to start.

THINKING 3D
Take-Away Thoughts

What can you do right now to start the process of living and Thinking 3D?

CONCLUSION

WHY NOT?

This is probably not the first leadership book you've ever read. But the truth is, there's no secret formula for success. There is no proven method or chart of statistics that can convince you or anyone else of what we're talking about.

There's just you.

You are the proven method when it comes to Thinking 3D. Changing the way your employees or coworkers think about their work starts with you. You will have to be the example.

HAVE YOU EVER BEEN to a motivational conference, read an inspiring book, or had a great vision about what your future could be? Did it last to a point where it truly changed your path forward? Most of the time it doesn't because we do nothing with it, and therefore it was simply a good thought or moment in time. We must challenge ourselves to instill Thinking 3D into our everyday lives purposefully in order to unlock the possibilities of what it can and will do for anyone who does so with absolute intention.

Remember, this journey is going to be lonely at first. Spreading these ideas around the office or warehouse is going to take time. People need to come to their own conclusions. They need to be allowed to push back. People need to see where they are on the map.

Look again at your company's "you are here" marker. It's going to look similar to a lot of businesses in this country.

Most of the current workforce has been born into a box. People get up, go to work, and put in the hours. After another mundane day they go home exhausted, unfulfilled, and disconnected to the people around them. Rinse and repeat.

Is this truly all there is to life and are we are supposed to merely accept it? The thoughts, ideas and principles in this book are seeds. You've already invested time and/or money reading up until this point; therefore you have purchased the seed. Does a farmer buy seed, throw it on the surface of the field and say "I'll be back in the fall to reap the harvest"? Of course not. The farmer knows the process and knows there is a reward for following it.

"A dime and a $20 gold piece have the same value if they are corroding at the bottom of the ocean. The difference in value is manifested only when you lift those coins up and use them as they were intended to be used."

– Major Reuben Siverling, former U.S. Army Captain

To get the maximum value out of the seed from Think 3D, you need to water it, protect it from the elements, fertilize it, and cultivate it in order to reap the harvest. Back to the principle of intention: odds are if you've gotten to this point of the book, you recognize to some level the opportunities around you.

Why are we neglecting our families and ignoring our coworkers? Why does work wipe us out, leaving little or nothing for the rest of our lives? Why can't we change these bad habits?

Is this the best employers can offer people? Is this the best we expect from and for ourselves?

To take action we must first truly decide. Decide that we deserve to make the most of this one life given to us. We should be challenged to ask the question, do we want to live with the pain of growth today, or the pain of regret years from now?

The reality is one cannot prosper beyond the confines of their highest aspiration. One cannot aspire to become something they don't believe is possible. Why not believe in the impossible?

Thinking outside the box isn't good enough anymore. We're talking about people's lives here. As far as we're concerned, there shouldn't even be a box.

From CEOs to entry-level employees, we are all looking for happiness. We must all acknowledge the impact our jobs have in this pursuit. It is time to challenge the conditioned thought process of "I can't" and "I shouldn't" and actually do something.

DON'T HATE THE WEIGHTS

- Very few people enjoy lifting weights. When you first start lifting, the following days you feel the soreness in your muscles. This is one of the many reasons people hate the weights. But to see success, you must look beyond the temporary and cling to the vision of where you want to be. The weights are merely a tool to help you obtain the shape you want to be in.

- Many people take this same thought process into the other areas of their life. They don't make changes or take risks because they think, "What if I step out and then feel pain?" Pain in life is going to come whether we take the step of faith or not. But those who leverage the weight of pain and discomfort reap the benefits of growth.

- Don't hate the weights; embrace them for what they can help you become.

> "There are no victories at bargain prices."
>
> – Dwight D. Eisenhower

If you're reading this, you are in a place where admitting "I'm okay with being average" does not feel right. The average person isn't satisfied in their work. The average worker doesn't have enough energy for their family at the end of the day. The average employee doesn't expect their employer to invest in their life.

You should not be satisfied with "average."

What do you plan on doing today that's going to make an impact in six months? That's right, six months. Breaking an old habit or learning a better one takes at least that much time to start working. Anything less would be temporary. Anything less would be average.

Everyone has the potential of greatness inside them just like every acorn has an oak tree inside it. Like any motivational book, *Think 3D* can't help anyone unless it is planted and nurtured. A good idea needs constant and intentional exposure to take root. And after that, it takes years to fully grow.

"The acorn has an oak tree in it, but if we just let that acorn lie around, the oak tree will never come to life. Now you have a choice - develop and use the seeds and bring your "oak tree" to full maturity, or let them lie around and watch your oak tree die."

– Zig Ziglar

> "In your hands you hold the seeds of failure - or the potential for greatness. Your hands are capable but they must be used - and for the right things - to reap the rewards you are capable of attaining."
>
> – Zig Ziglar

Choose to become completely determined to invest in what *Think 3D* can give you. Each of us is the master of our own destiny. Every day we have choices in front of us that will shape the future of our lives. When we're determined to put to use what we've learned, put into action the principles of intent and exposure, we'll start creating the best life possible for ourselves.

Remember: Thinking 3D is about making people happier.

We believe change is possible in your business culture. You deserve to be happy and so do your coworkers. When that is the drive behind change, people will begin to take notice.

We wish you the best of luck and God's blessings in bringing this joy into your business.

THINKING 3D
Take-Away Thoughts
Why Not?

THINK 3D | 121

Tamien Dysart

Vaney Hariri

ABOUT THE AUTHORS

Tamien Dysart and Vaney Hariri have collectively worked with several Fortune 500 financial companies for over 30 years. They continue to demonstrate a highly successful track record of developing and implementing strategies and programs which build and sustain high-performing cultures. They have been instrumental in driving high levels of associate engagement while producing best-in-class performance and customer satisfaction results. Their proven proficiency in leadership development is at the core of what has led to their success within numerous cultural environments.

p. (605) 521-2637
e. tamien@think3d.solutions
e. vaney@think3d.solutions

Think3D
2329 N. Career Ave.
Sioux Falls, SD 57107